Zack Packs a Snack

by Liza Charlesworth • illustrated by Jim Paillot

SCHOLASTIC INC.

New York • Toronto • London • Auckland
Sydney • Mexico City • New Delhi • Hong Kong

Designed by Grafica, Inc.
ISBN: 978-0-545-68627-3
Copyright © 2009 by Lefty's Editorial Services.

12 11 10 9 8 7 6 5 4 3 2 1   68   15 16 17 18 19 20/0

Printed in China.

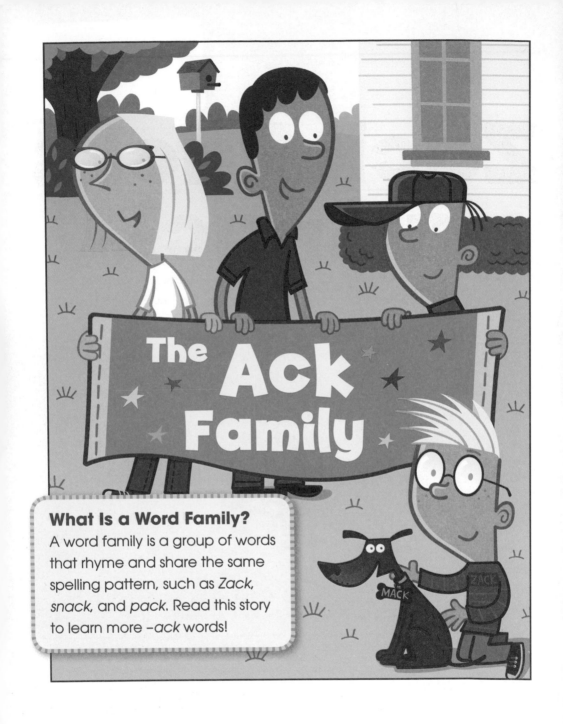

What Is a Word Family?
A word family is a group of words that rhyme and share the same spelling pattern, such as *Zack*, *snack*, and *pack*. Read this story to learn more –*ack* words!

Meet **Zack**.
Zack is a member of the **Ack** family.

Zack lives with his mom, dad,
and brother, **Jack**.
He also lives with his dog named **Mack**.

Zack has a **knack**
for making zany **snack**s.
Want to see?

Zack takes some bread
and adds a **stack** of ham.

Zack adds a **stack** of cheese.

Zack adds a **stack** of **crack**ers.

Zack adds pickles and **black** olives
and a whole **pack** of jelly beans.

Zack packs his **snack** in a **sack**
and goes to get his **jack**et from the **rack**.
Picnic time!

But when **Zack** gets **back**,
the **sack** is gone!

Who took **Zack**'s **sack**?
Not **Mom** or **Dad** or brother **Jack**.
They do not like **Zack**'s zany **snack**s.

Then **Zack** sees some muddy **track**s . . .

which lead him to a little **shack**.
It was **Mack** who took **Zack**'s **snack**!
And it was way too late to get it **back**.

Word Family House

Point to the *-ack* word in each room and read it aloud.

back	sack	lack
pack	tack	quack
rack	Zack	black
snack		knack
smack		shack

Word Family Riddles

Read each -*ack* riddle. Then point to the answer in the word box.

1 I am a color.

2 I am what a train rides on.

3 I am what a duck says.

4 I am a bag.

5 I am a little meal.

WORD BOX

snack

black

sack

quack

track

Word Family Bingo

Which words belong to the *-ack* family? Cover them with buttons or pennies. Get four in a row to win!

mug	chin	shack	chug
clam	tack	stack	hot
back	lack	rack	snack
will	pack	tot	pug

Answer: Bingo is the third row across: back, lack, rack, snack.